Words for Worship

Words for Worship

Prayers from the heart of the
Church of England

Compiled and edited by

Gill Ambrose, Anders Bergquist,
Paul Bradshaw, Christopher Irvine,
David Kennedy, Colin Podmore,
Christopher Woods

**Transforming
Worship**

Living the new creation

The Liturgical Commission

Church House Publishing
Church House
Great Smith Street
London
SW1P 3AZ

ISBN 978 0 7151 2190 0

Published 2012 by Church House Publishing
Copyright © Archbishops' Council 2012

Email: copyright@churchofengland.org.uk

Common Worship is copyright © The Archbishops' Council, 2000–2008.
Material from this work is reproduced with permission.

Extracts from the *Book of Common Prayer*, the rights in which are vested
in the Crown, are reproduced by permission of the Crown's Patentee,
Cambridge University Press.

Typeset by RefineCatch Limited, Bungay, Suffolk
Printed in England by CPI Group (UK), Croydon

Contents

Preface
by the Archbishop of Canterbury

Over the last decade or so, the Church of England has sought to move a bit out of its comfort zones, in order to engage more with people where they are. And where they are, of course, is most often quite a long way away from the world in which the language of the Church's public worship is familiar. The easy reaction would be to say simply that we need to start from scratch, take nothing for granted and produce completely new material. There is certainly room for new material; but it is crucial not to cut ourselves off from the heritage of words and forms that have held the love and aspiration of so many Christians of earlier ages. If we take people really seriously, we should be ready to give them something to grow into. So the less easy but no less creative response to our situation is to try and introduce this heritage in accessible and sensitive ways.

So many congregations find that this meets an urgent need: not long ago, I was given by the leader of a large independent black-led church of Pentecostal tradition his own book on ancient forms of prayer and devotion, a fine collection of the sort of material that, he said, his people were hungry for. And here we have this task performed for our own Anglican tradition in a book that draws together not only the words of prayers inherited from our Christian forebears but the underlying rationale of the shape of the Christian Year and the basic structures of liturgy, along with lucid and straightforward accounts of how prayer and liturgy got to be the way they are, and some very helpful indications about where to look for the biblical roots of so much of what we say in public prayer.

Acknowledging that many who are coming to our churches – especially to 'fresh expressions' of church life – have little or no background in the old forms of worship doesn't mean that we have to patronize them or deny them the wealth that is there, out of a well-meaning but mistaken wish not to make things difficult. As men and women grow in love and understanding

Words for Worship

for God, they will need more and more resources to carry their thoughts and feelings and to feed their imaginations. This book offers material that has stood the test of time in Christian experience, and promises to enrich the discipleship of all who use these words. I am delighted to see its publication.

+ Rowan Cantuar:

Introduction

Christians pray: sometimes by themselves and sometimes together; day by day, week by week, Sunday by Sunday; at the Eucharist and at morning and evening prayer; at baptisms, weddings, funerals, ordinations and other great occasions in life. Over the centuries, they have built up a treasure-store of prayers for use in shared worship, and this book presents a selection of prayers that are especially cherished in the worship of the Church of England.

Who is this collection for?

We hope that this selection will help at least:

- Those who already worship regularly at Church of England services, and would like to know more about the origin and background of words that are familiar.
- Those who are new to Anglican worship, for whom the book provides a tour of some of the main landmarks of the liturgy.
- Those who would like a selection of prayers that can be learned by heart.

Where do these texts come from?

All the texts in this book are commonly used in the Church of England's public worship, though not all of them began as texts written for the liturgy. Many of them are combinations and recasting of the words of Scripture, because the most durable Christian prayers are always those that are deeply grounded in the Bible. Some of these prayers originated in the Church of England, but many go back to medieval or early Christian times. Since the Church of England understands itself to be an expression of the universal or catholic Church, it is hardly surprising that most of the prayers in a collection of its most central worship texts will be made up of words that were shaped long before the Church of England had asserted its own identity within western Christianity.

Some of the prayers in this book were originally written in Greek and Latin, the two main languages of early Christian worship, but they have become so familiar in the English language that it is hard to remember that they are translations or adaptations at all. Sometimes these translations have been agreed with other English-speaking churches, including ones outside the Anglican Communion.

Most of the texts in this book reveal the characteristic shape of Christian prayer, which is offered to God the Father, through Jesus Christ his Son, and in the power of the Holy Spirit who inspires our prayer. This Trinitarian shape comes out both in the body of the prayers and in the way in which many of them end. And although almost all these texts are addressed to God in the form of prayer, they also express the Church's teaching about God, Christ and the world. There is a traditional Latin saying, *lex orandi, lex credendi* – roughly translated as 'the way we pray is the way we believe' – and the Church of England in particular has seen its teaching as being embedded in its liturgies, rather than in formal statements of belief.

How is this book structured?

The prayers in this book are divided into nine sections.

Basics introduces four texts, beginning with the prayer that Jesus himself taught to his disciples.

Responses consists of short exchanges commonly used at services, where a speaker, usually the 'president', 'officiant' or 'celebrant' (that is, the person who leads and holds together the act of worship), invites a response from the congregation (that is, the people who have gathered to worship). There are many ways in which the congregation take part in the worship. They may take part silently, in their hearts, as prayers are said or sung by someone else (perhaps a choir). The president may speak the words on everyone's behalf, and the people then make that prayer their own by saying 'Amen' at the end. And sometimes, as in responses, there is a short dialogue between one person and the congregation.

Holy Communion: some main texts introduces prayers that are especially found in the principal Christian act of worship, also known as the Eucharist or the Lord's Supper.

Prayers of Preparation, Penitence and Thanksgiving reminds us that Jesus came to call his hearers to repent and that those who are truly sorry for what they have done will discover the love and mercy of God. Every main Christian act of worship takes us on the journey through repentance to the assurance of sins forgiven.

The Nicene Creed, which is recited at Holy Communion on Sundays and principal holy days, is given a section of its own. Like the Apostles' Creed – the other statement of shared belief that is commonly recited in Anglican worship – the Nicene Creed reminds us of the way in which words for worship are also words that express the church's teaching.

Gospel Canticles presents a collection of passages of Scripture that are used as 'songs of praise', especially at Morning and Evening Prayer.

Prayers from the **Book of Common Prayer (BCP)** contains a selection of well-loved prayers from the 1662 Prayer Book.

The BCP also contains 'collects' for every Sunday and main festival of the Church's year; these are short prayers in which the president gathers up or 'collects' the prayers of the people. *Classic collects* offers a small selection.

Modern collects for each season is a parallel selection of collects from *Common Worship*, the Church of England's present-day liturgical library.

The layout of the prayers in this book

Often, the prayers are printed in two forms, one above the other or side by side. The one printed first, or on the left-hand side, is the one found in the modern-language provision in *Common Worship*. The one printed below, or on the right-hand side, is from the *Book of Common Prayer*, or (when this particular prayer is not found in the BCP) from the traditional language provision in *Common Worship*.

Each text is introduced with a comment on its meaning and its particular significance in worship, and with some indication of its history. Some technical terms, or names of particular service books, are highlighted in **bold**. These words are further explained in *Where do words for our worship come from?* and the *Glossary* at the end of the book (pp. **53–8**).

In modern-language prayer books, including *Common Worship*, it is usual for prayers to be printed out in lines according to sense-units. This is called 'lining out'.

The *Book of Common Prayer* does not use lining out. Instead it prints prayers as blocks of text, using complex punctuation and capital letters to mark the sense-units. In the case of **canticles**, it also uses a colon in place of normal punctuation to separate the two halves of each verse. These indicate the right place to pause and breathe when the canticle is used in worship; *Common Worship* uses a small red diamond to do the same job.

In this book, which is not designed to be used in worship, and where it is helpful to be able to compare modern language and traditional language versions of the same prayer easily, neither the colons nor the red diamonds are used, and all the prayers are lined out. Capitals and punctuation have then been adjusted as necessary. But the words of the prayers from the *Book of Common Prayer* have otherwise been left as they are, as have those capital letters that appear in the body of the text that have a theological significance, such as 'thy holy Name', 'according to the Scriptures', 'thy Divine Majesty'.

1

Basics

1.1 The Lord's Prayer

Our Father in heaven,
hallowed be your name,
your kingdom come
your will be done,
on earth as in heaven.
Give us today our daily bread.
Forgive us our sins
as we forgive those who sin against us.
Lead us not into temptation
but deliver us from evil.
For the kingdom, the power,
and the glory are yours
now and for ever.
Amen.

Our Father, who art in heaven,
hallowed be thy name;
thy kingdom come;
thy will be done;
on earth as it is in heaven.
Give us this day our daily bread.
And forgive us our trespasses,
as we forgive those who trespass against us.
And lead us not into temptation;
but deliver us from evil.
For thine is the kingdom,
the power and the glory,
for ever and ever.
Amen.

From *Common Worship*

Words for Worship

This is the prayer that Jesus taught his disciples, when they asked him how they should pray. Most Christians know the prayer by heart in their own language, and it is used today by every Christian tradition, though there are sometimes minor variations in the wording. It has a place in every Anglican act of worship, and forms a pattern for prayer for Christians: we bless God and pray for God's will to prevail on earth; we pray for daily needs to be met, for forgiveness for wrongdoings, strength to resist temptation and protection from danger.

The text is found in two slightly different versions in the New Testament – Matthew 6.9–13 and Luke 11.2–4. The prayer as we use it today is a version that was adapted by the early Christian communities from the two Gospel texts, and it was taught in this form to new converts. The final sentence, giving glory to God, is called the **doxology**. It is not part of the New Testament text, but was added very early on. The Lord's Prayer is occasionally said without it.

The Lord's Prayer is printed in the *Book of Common Prayer* in a form slightly different from what is often called the 'traditional' form printed above. Here the variations are shown in italics:

Our Father, *which* art in heaven,
hallowed be thy name;
thy kingdom come;
thy will be done;
***in* earth as it is in heaven.**
Give us this day our daily bread.
And forgive us our trespasses,
as we forgive *them that* trespass against us.
And lead us not into temptation;
but deliver us from evil.
For thine is the kingdom,
the power and the glory,
for ever and ever.
Amen.

1.2 The Apostles' Creed

I believe in God, the Father almighty,
creator of heaven and earth.

I believe in Jesus Christ, his only Son, our Lord,
who was conceived by the Holy Spirit,
born of the Virgin Mary,
suffered under Pontius Pilate,
was crucified, died, and was buried;
he descended to the dead.
On the third day he rose again;
he ascended into heaven,
he is seated at the right hand of the Father,
and he will come to judge the living and the dead.

I believe in the Holy Spirit,
the holy catholic Church,
the communion of saints,
the forgiveness of sins,
the resurrection of the body,
and the life everlasting.
Amen.

I believe in God the Father Almighty,
maker of heaven and earth:

and in Jesus Christ his only Son our Lord,
who was conceived by the Holy Ghost,
born of the Virgin Mary,
suffered under Pontius Pilate,
was crucified, dead, and buried.
He descended into hell;
the third day he rose again from the dead;
he ascended into heaven,
and sitteth on the right hand of God the Father Almighty;
from thence he shall come to judge the quick and the dead.

I believe in the Holy Ghost;
the holy Catholick Church;
the communion of saints;
the forgiveness of sins;
the resurrection of the body,
and the life everlasting.
Amen.

This statement of what Christians believe was taught to people who were preparing for baptism in the early centuries of the Christian Church. It became known as the Apostles' Creed, because it was thought to include the essential teaching of the 12 apostles, Jesus' earliest followers. It was into that faith of the apostles that Christians were, and are, baptized.

The Apostles' Creed is therefore a summary of what the Church teaches, and of what Christians together believe, rather than a detailed statement of individual and personal belief. Saying the Creed binds Christians together as a believing community, across different traditions and practices. As we say the Creed, we join Christians past and present, and from all over the world, in proclaiming our common faith. The Apostles' Creed is used especially at services of baptism and confirmation, and also when a creed is used at celebrations of Morning and Evening Prayer.

1.3 The Grace
The grace of our Lord Jesus Christ,
and the love of God,
and the fellowship of the Holy Spirit,
be with us all evermore.
Amen.

The grace of our Lord Jesus Christ,
and the love of God,
and the fellowship of the Holy Ghost,
be with us all, evermore.
Amen.

In these words, Christians bless one another and rejoice together in the shared experience of God's love, grace and communion, which involves all three persons of the Trinity: Father, Son and Holy Spirit. By saying the words together, Christians also affirm their commitment to one another. The words may be used in various settings. They are often a shared conclusion to prayers offered by a worship leader during a service, or as a prayerful conclusion to a meeting or gathering. People sometimes bow their heads in prayer as they say the words of the Grace but they may also look around the group and acknowledge one another's presence. The Grace is also used as a greeting at the beginning of a service or meeting.

The words of the Grace are those with which St Paul ends his Second Letter to the Corinthians (2 Corinthians 13.13). They have been used in their English form from the time of the Reformation.

In the *Book of Common Prayer* the words 'Holy Ghost' are used rather than 'Holy Spirit'.

In sixteenth-century English, the word 'ghost' does not mean what it usually means today. 'Ghost' is the equivalent of 'spirit': so 'ghostly counsel' means 'spiritual advice', and the 'Holy Ghost' is the *Book of Common Prayer*'s usual way of saying 'Holy Spirit'.

1.4 *'Glory to the Father...'*

Glory to the Father and to the Son
and to the Holy Spirit;
as it was in the beginning, is now
and shall be for ever. Amen.

Glory be to the Father, and to the Son,
and to the Holy Ghost;
as it was in the beginning is now,
and ever shall be:
world without end. Amen.

These words are often known as the **doxology**, or *Gloria Patri*, or simply as the *Gloria* – although this last runs a risk of confusion with *Gloria in excelsis* [4.11 below], which is also commonly called the *Gloria*.

Since early Christian times, *Gloria Patri* has been added to the end of an Old Testament psalm or **canticle**, when a text from the Hebrew Bible is used by a Christian community to worship God.

The Book of Psalms has a particular dynamism among the books of the Bible. The psalms began as human words addressed to God, words that contain an immense range of poetry, praise, lament, distress and serenity. Incorporated into the books of the Bible, they become part of God's word to us. In worship, they become our words to God again. The first Christians, being Jewish, were already familiar with the use of the psalms in worship, but they came to use them in a new way, as songs about the Christ. Later Christians therefore added this ending, as we still do today when we pray God's word back to God the Father, through Christ the Son, in the power of the Holy Spirit.

2

Responses

In church services there are often moments when the person leading the service says something to which a reply from the congregation might be expected. In ordinary life, the greeting 'Good morning' normally invites a 'Good morning' in response. This section introduces some of the 'responses' most often used in worship.

2.1 An opening greeting

The Lord be with you
and also with you.

From Easter Day to Pentecost this acclamation follows

Alleluia. Christ is risen.
He is risen indeed. Alleluia.

The Lord be with you
and with thy spirit.

Opening an act of worship with these words enables the worship leader, and those gathered together, to greet each other in the name of the Lord, and to affirm God's presence among them. During the seven weeks from Easter Day to Pentecost, which together make up the Easter season, the special acclamation is added, as Christians share with one another with particular vividness their joy at the resurrection of Jesus. In the version of the greeting in the *Book of Common Prayer*, 'spirit' is a reference to what each of us fundamentally is as a human person: it does not mean 'spirit' as contrasted with 'body'.

2.2 After a reading

This is the word of the Lord.
Thanks be to God.

The custom of making a thankful response after a reading from Scripture seems to have originated in the early Middle Ages. More recently, this response has come to be 'cued' by words from the reader, who reminds the listeners of the significance of what they have heard. It may feel hard to say this response when it follows a challenging reading, or one of the darker stories in the Bible, but it is said just the same: to show that these demanding passages also have to be wrestled with, as part of Scripture.

2.3 Responses to the Gospel reading

Hear the Gospel of our Lord Jesus Christ according to *N.*
Glory to you, O Lord.

This is the Gospel of the Lord.
Praise to you, O Christ.

Hear the Gospel of our Lord Jesus Christ according to N.

or: The holy Gospel is written in...

Glory be to thee, O Lord.

This is the Gospel of the Lord.
Praise be to thee, O Christ.

From *Common Worship*

There is always a reading from one of the Gospels at a service of Holy Communion. Although in early Christian centuries people probably stood for the greater part of the service, they took special care to stand during the reading of the Gospel, as it often included the words of Jesus himself. The words of introduction reminded the congregation of the significance of what was about to be read, and the congregation, by standing and offering praise, showed that they were actively engaged with the words of the Gospel, and with the minister who was reading them. Similarly, the reader notes the end of the passage, and the people show by their response that they are not passive observers, but active hearers of the word.

2.4 A response to prayer for others

Lord, in your mercy
hear our prayer.

Lord, in thy mercy
hear our prayer.

Lord, hear us.
Lord, graciously hear us.

O Lord, hear our prayer
**and let our cry come
unto thee.**

From *Common Worship*

These words are used to help worshippers to participate in thanksgiving and prayers for others (often called **intercessions**). The response enables the congregation to affirm the prayers as their own. The petition 'O Lord, hear our prayer, and let our cry come unto thee' is taken from Psalm 102.1.

2.5 The Peace

The peace of the Lord be always with you
and also with you.

The peace of the Lord be always with you
and with thy spirit.

From *Common Worship*

Christians have always greeted each other in the name of the Lord, to celebrate and proclaim their belonging together to Christ. The New Testament letters, which give us glimpses of the life of early Christian communities, speak of Christians greeting one another with a 'holy kiss' (cf. Romans 16.16, 2 Corinthians 13.12), as a sign of being brothers and sisters in Christ. This later became known as the 'kiss of peace'. It was a sign of reconciliation among those who gathered for worship, and a reminder that true peace is found in Christ. As time went by, words were added to the action, and are still used when Christians exchange a sign of peace. The words echo the risen

Jesus' greeting to his disciples: 'Peace be with you' (John 20.19). In recent times, it has become customary to shake hands at the peace, but the words can be used without this gesture.

In the early Middle Ages, it became customary for clergy alone to exchange the kiss of peace, but from the eleventh century a substitute was introduced for lay people. An object called the pax, or 'pax-brede' ('peace-board'), was passed around the members of the congregation for them to kiss in turn. The pax was usually a smooth round disk made of wood or precious metal, and was often fashioned to resemble the eucharistic bread. A sacred emblem, such as the Crucifix or Lamb of God, was usually painted on it. At a time when lay people received Holy Communion very rarely, the kissing of the pax was one of the main actions that members of the congregation shared in, and it helped to unite them into a corporate body.

2.6 When receiving Holy Communion

The body of Christ
Amen.

[A] The Body of our Lord Jesus Christ, which was given for thee, preserve thy body and soul unto everlasting life. [B] Take and eat this in remembrance that Christ died for thee, and feed on him in thy heart by faith with thanksgiving.

The blood of Christ
Amen.

[A] The Blood of our Lord Jesus Christ, which was shed for thee, preserve thy body and soul unto everlasting life. [B] Drink this in remembrance that Christ's Blood was shed for thee, and be thankful.

The shorter form of words has been used at the giving of Holy Communion at least since the fourth century, and probably long before that. Today, further words may be added, such as 'The body of Christ, given for you.' The longer form of words has a more complex history. Those marked [A] are an English translation from medieval Latin, and were used in the **1549 Prayer Book**. Those marked [B] replaced those marked [A] in the **1552 Prayer Book**, and were intended to encourage a more strongly reformed understanding of Holy Communion. In the **1559 Prayer Book**, the [A] words and the [B] words were combined, and they are found in combination in all subsequent editions of the *Book of Common Prayer*.

The words at the giving of Holy Communion are all ultimately drawn from the New Testament accounts of the Last Supper, at which Jesus said to his disciples: 'This is my body', 'This is my blood' and 'Do this in remembrance of me' (Matthew 26.26–28, Luke 22.19–20, 1 Corinthians 11.24–25). Holy Communion has to be received as a gift, and not just given or taken. In saying 'Amen', those who receive the bread and the wine show that they recognize Christ's gift of himself through them.

2.7 A conclusion or ending

Let us bless the Lord.
Thanks be to God.

These words are often used to offer praise to God at the end of a service. They reflect the many words in the Psalms that urge God's people to bless the Lord, and the many thanksgivings in the letters of St Paul. Just as it is important for worshippers to greet one another at the start of a service, so they need a way to mark the ending. In this short response, they acknowledge together their gratitude to God, as the final words of a community that has been gathered for praise.

2.8 A dismissal or sending-out

Go in peace to love and serve the Lord.
In the name of Christ. Amen.

Go in the peace of Christ.
Thanks be to God.

From Easter Day to Pentecost

Go in the peace of Christ. Alleluia, Alleluia.
Thanks be to God. Alleluia, Alleluia.

Words for Worship

At the end of an act of worship, Christians are, and always have been, commissioned to carry out God's purpose in their lives in the everyday world. This is every Christian's mission. Worship is not simply a get-together of like-minded people focused on God. Its purpose is to transform us, so that the message of God's love for humanity, shown in Christ, will influence our everyday encounters and relationships. The people respond with gratitude to their commission. In the weeks of Easter, the word 'Alleluia' is added to remind people to go in special joy, full of the life of the risen Christ.

In the Latin service of early and medieval times, the dismissal was '*Ite, missa est*', literally 'Go, it is sent.' This is the origin of the word 'Mass' as an alternative name for the **Eucharist**.

3

Holy Communion: some main texts

3.1 Kyrie eleison

Kyrie eleison.
Christe eleison.
Kyrie eleison.

Kyrie eleison.
Christe eleison.
Kyrie eleison.

Lord, have mercy.
Christ, have mercy.
Lord, have mercy.

Lord, have mercy upon us.
Christ, have mercy upon us.
Lord, have mercy upon us.

The Greek words, *Kyrie eleison, Christe eleison*, mean literally 'Lord, have mercy; Christ have mercy'. The *'Kyries'* (as they are popularly known) are most usually said or sung as responses during the prayers of penitence at Holy Communion, but they can also be used as responses in the prayers of **intercession**.

Kyrie eleison was a response to a series of intercessory petitions (and could perhaps be better translated as 'Lord, mercifully hear us'). In time, the prayer petitions were dropped in the **Roman rite**, leaving only the responses, which were said as part of the introductory prayers of the Eucharist. The *Kyries* are usually used in multiples of three.

The continued use of this Greek text is a living link with our Christian origins. The earliest Christian communities worshipped in the Greek language, and even when Latin had replaced Greek as the usual language of worship in the Christian west, the *Kyries* continued to be said in Greek. In Anglican use, they are regularly said in either Greek or English.

3.2 Sursum corda

The Lord be with you
and also with you.
(or)
The Lord is here.
His Spirit is with us.

Lift up your hearts.
We lift them to the Lord.

Let us give thanks to the Lord our God.
It is right to give thanks and praise.

[The Lord be with you
and with thy spirit.]

Lift up your hearts.
We lift them up unto the Lord.

Let us give thanks unto the Lord our God.
It is meet and right so to do.

The dialogue that introduces the eucharistic prayer is known as *Sursum corda* (literally, 'up hearts' in Latin). This dialogue has been used almost universally since at least the third century, and continuously in Anglican worship since the Reformation. It is found in both a shorter and a longer form, with or without its opening greeting. Cranmer kept the greeting in the **1549 Prayer Book** but dropped it in **1552**; it was reintroduced in the **1928 Prayer Book**.

These words express the truth that the focus of worship is heaven itself, where Christ reigns. Christian worship is the meeting of heaven and earth, as we join 'with angels and archangels and all the company of heaven'.

Thanksgiving is at the very heart of Christian living. The invitation, 'Let *us* give thanks to the Lord our God', underlines the fact that the eucharistic prayer, the great prayer of thanksgiving, is the prayer of the whole assembly in which everyone shares, even when they are not speaking the words.

3.3 Sanctus and Benedictus qui venit

Holy, holy, holy Lord,
God of power and might,
heaven and earth are full of your glory.
Hosanna in the highest.
Blessed is he who comes in the name of the Lord.
Hosanna in the highest.

Holy, holy, holy, Lord God of hosts,
heaven and earth are full of thy glory.
Glory be to thee, O Lord most High.

[Blessed is he that cometh in the name of the Lord.
Hosanna in the highest.]

The *Sanctus* and *Benedictus qui venit* (from the Latin for 'holy' and 'blessed is he who comes') are two short chants that are used during the eucharistic prayer as a congregational response to the words of thanksgiving said by the priest. The priest praises God for his mighty acts of creation and redemption, and then invites the congregation to join with angels and archangels in the song of heaven, which is the *Sanctus*. Cranmer kept it in the **1549 Prayer Book** but dropped it in **1552**; it was reintroduced in the **1928 Prayer Book**.

The words of the *Sanctus* are those of the seraphs, or heavenly beings, heard by the prophet Isaiah in a mystical experience (Isaiah 6.3). Their adoption by Christians may derive from their use in Jewish worship. The *Sanctus* has been used in this way since at least the fourth century, and it is found in the eucharistic prayers of nearly all Christian traditions.

The words of *Benedictus qui venit* are from Psalm 118.26. They were used by the crowd that welcomed Jesus when he entered Jerusalem on a donkey in the week before he was crucified. By using the words at this point in the Eucharist, we proclaim the fact that Jesus comes to us today in Holy Communion. The *Benedictus* is not as widely used as the *Sanctus*.

'Hosanna in the highest' is drawn from the same Psalm (118.25). The Hebrew word *Hosanna* was both a plea ('O Lord, save us') and a joyful acclamation of praise to God, who dwells in the highest heaven. Both meanings are important, as we rejoice in Christ who is our Saviour, and whom we worship as Messiah and Lord.

3.4 Agnus Dei

Lamb of God,	O Lamb of God,
you take away the sin of the world,	that takest away
have mercy on us.	the sins of the world,
	have mercy upon us.
Lamb of God,	
you take away the sin of the world,	O Lamb of God,
have mercy on us.	that takest away
	the sins of the world,
Lamb of God,	have mercy upon us.
you take away the sin of the world,	
grant us peace.	O Lamb of God,
	that takest away
	the sins of the world,
	grant us thy peace.
	From *Common Worship*

Agnus Dei (Latin for 'Lamb of God') is a chant said or sung before the distribution of Holy Communion. It is a direct address to Christ: a warmly devotional expression of the belief that here we encounter the risen Christ himself. The request, 'have mercy upon us', arises directly from our conviction that it is Christ himself who makes atonement for our sin by his sacrifice of himself on the cross, while the final petition, 'grant us peace', testifies to the grace and peace of sins forgiven.

The words come from John the Baptist's testimony to Christ, 'Behold, the Lamb of God, who takes away the sin of the world' (John 1.29, 36). They were introduced into the **Roman rite** from the eastern churches in the seventh century, when the chant was repeated while the eucharistic breads were being broken for distribution. In the same way, *Common Worship* (Order One) says that 'the Agnus Dei may be used as the bread is broken.' In the **1549 Prayer Book** the Agnus Dei is to be sung 'during communion time', but Cranmer dropped it in **1552**. It was reintroduced in the **1928 Prayer Book**.

4

Prayers of Preparation, Penitence and Thanksgiving

4.1 The Collect for Purity

Almighty God
to whom all hearts are open,
all desires known,
and from whom no secrets are hidden:
cleanse the thoughts of our hearts
by the inspiration of your Holy Spirit,
that we may perfectly love you,
and worthily magnify your holy name,
through Christ our Lord. Amen.

Almighty God,
unto whom all hearts be open,
all desires known,
and from whom no secrets are hid:
cleanse the thoughts of our hearts
by the inspiration of thy Holy Spirit,
that we may perfectly love thee,
and worthily magnify thy holy Name;
through Christ our Lord. Amen.

As we gather with others to offer the Church's prayer and praise, we invoke the Holy Spirit, asking that God's life may breathe through us, that we may voice our prayers and sing God's praise. We can only pray in and through the Holy Spirit; as Saint Paul says, it is the Spirit who prays in us, and the God to whom our prayers are addressed knows us better than we know ourselves (Romans 8.26–27).

Words for Worship

When we gather to celebrate the Eucharist, we long to receive what Christ wants to give to us. The accent in this Prayer of Preparation therefore falls on our being open to welcome and to receive the Word – Christ who seeks to come and dwell with us, as Jesus invited himself to be the dinner guest at the table of Zacchaeus (Luke 19.1–10).

This concisely expressed prayer has a long history in English liturgical books. Scholars believe that it was composed around 780 by Abbot Gregory of St Augustine's Abbey, Canterbury. In the **Sarum rite**, the prayer was part of the preparation said in Latin by the priest before going to the altar to offer the Mass. Cranmer made it the opening prayer of the Holy Communion service in the **1549 Prayer Book**, and it remained in that position in the **1662 Prayer Book**. It was then to be said by the priest alone; today it is more commonly said by the whole of the congregation together.

4.2 The Ten Commandments

God spake these words, and said; I am the Lord thy God: Thou shalt have none other gods but me.

Lord, have mercy upon us, and incline our hearts to keep this law.

Thou shalt not make to thyself any graven image, nor the likeness of any thing that is in heaven above, or in the earth beneath, or in the water under the earth. Thou shalt not bow down to them, nor worship them: for I the Lord thy God am a jealous God, and visit the sins of the fathers upon the children unto the third and fourth generation of them that hate me, and shew mercy unto thousands in them that love me, and keep my commandments.

Lord, have mercy upon us, and incline our hearts to keep this law.

Thou shalt not take the Name of the Lord thy God in vain: for the Lord will not hold him guiltless, that taketh his Name in vain.

Lord, have mercy upon us, and incline our hearts to keep this law.

Remember that thou keep holy the Sabbath-day. Six days shalt thou labour, and do all that thou hast to do; but the seventh day is the

Sabbath of the Lord thy God. In it thou shalt do no manner of work, thou, and thy son, and thy daughter, thy man-servant, and thy maid-servant, thy cattle, and the stranger that is within thy gates. For in six days the Lord made heaven and earth, the sea, and all that in them is, and rested the seventh day: wherefore the Lord blessed the seventh day, and hallowed it.

Lord, have mercy upon us, and incline our hearts to keep this law.

Honour thy father and thy mother; that thy days may be long in the land which the Lord thy God giveth thee.

Lord, have mercy upon us, and incline our hearts to keep this law.

Thou shalt do no murder.

Lord, have mercy upon us, and incline our hearts to keep this law.

Thou shalt not commit adultery.

Lord, have mercy upon us, and incline our hearts to keep this law.

Thou shalt not steal.

Lord, have mercy upon us, and incline our hearts to keep this law.

Thou shalt not bear false witness against thy neighbour.

Lord, have mercy upon us, and incline our hearts to keep this law.

Thou shalt not covet thy neighbour's house, thou shalt not covet thy neighbour's wife, nor his servant, nor his maid, nor his ox, nor his ass, nor any thing that is his.

Lord, have mercy upon us, and write all these thy laws in our hearts, we beseech thee.

(This is the text of the Ten Commandments as it is printed in the *Book of Common Prayer*, at the beginning of the service of Holy Communion. A shorter modern-language version may be found on p.162 of *Common Worship*.)

Following a precedent set by some earlier Reformers, the Ten Commandments (from Exodus 20.2–17) were introduced into the **1552 Prayer Book**, with expanded *Kyrie* responses, to provide a penitential preparation for the service. They continued to have this role in later revisions. In the **1928 Prayer Book**, a shorter form was substituted, and the Summary of the Law (4.3 below) and the *Kyries* were added as alternatives. **Series 1** allowed either the shorter or the longer form; from **Series 2** onwards, the Ten Commandments were moved to an appendix at the end of the service. In *Common Worship*, they have been moved to the very beginning, where they form part of an optional form of preparation for the Eucharist.

The congregational response, 'Lord, have mercy upon us, and incline our hearts to keep this law', recognizes that we are not able to live in God's way by our own strength, but only through his grace. It echoes another Old Testament passage in which the prophet Jeremiah looked forward to a new ordering of relationships, when God's law would be inscribed directly on the human heart, to direct the choices we make and the things we seek to do (Jeremiah 31.33).

4.3 The Summary of the Law

Our Lord Jesus Christ said:
The first commandment is this:
'Hear, O Israel,
The Lord our God is the only Lord.
You shall love the Lord your God
with all your heart,
with all your soul,
with all your mind,
and with all your strength.'

The second is this:
'Love your neighbour as yourself.'
There is no other commandment greater than these.
On these two commandments hang all the law and the prophets.

Amen. Lord, have mercy.

Our Lord Jesus Christ said:
Hear, O Israel.
The Lord our God is one Lord;
and thou shalt love the Lord thy God
with all thy heart,
and with all thy soul,
and with all thy mind,
and with all thy strength.
This is the first commandment.

And the second is like, namely this:
Thou shalt love thy neighbour as thyself.
There is none other commandment greater than these.
On these two commandments hang all the law and the prophets.

**Lord, have mercy upon us,
and write all these thy laws in our hearts, we beseech thee.**

When we come before God in worship, we are to bring our whole selves, and all that makes us who we are. Worship itself is the expression of our love for God, and this love for God also means that we are to love all that God loves, as God loves. Love is both the motive and meaning of our Christian lives: as St Paul says, 'the love of Christ compels us' (2 Corinthians 5.14).

In response to a question about the greatest commandment (Matthew 22.37–40 and Mark 12.29–31) Jesus replied by quoting two texts from the Hebrew Bible: Deuteronomy 6.5, and Leviticus 19.18. The common element in these texts is love: the love of God and the love of neighbour. The *torah*, or law of God, was seen as the gift of God to his people Israel, and it taught the people how to live according to the will and purposes of God. In the **1928 Prayer Book**, the Summary of the Law was included as an alternative to the recitation of all of the Ten Commandments.

4.4 'Almighty God, our heavenly Father...'

Almighty God, our heavenly Father,
we have sinned against you
and against our neighbour
in thought and word and deed,
through negligence, through weakness,
through our own deliberate fault.
We are truly sorry
and repent of all our sins.
For the sake of your Son Jesus Christ,
who died for us,
forgive us all that is past
and grant that we may serve you in newness of life
to the glory of your name. Amen.

This is a modern prayer for the shared confession of sins during the Eucharist (first used in the **Series 2** Holy Communion Service). It is usually said at the beginning of the service, as part of the Gathering, during which the congregation are called again to be the people of God, who through baptism turn away from sin and seek to live in the light of Christ.

When we gather with others for worship, we recognize that our sin not only consists in individual faults and failures, but also results from our shared human condition. The word 'sin' has a bad press, and some might prefer not to use the word at all. But if we are to be honest with ourselves, and realistic about the kind of world in which we live, then the concept of sin is unavoidable. The New Testament word for sin, *hamartia*, has a sense of 'missing the mark', falling short of what God expects of us. This prayer includes the expression of sorrow for our deliberate sin – those occasions when we have acted in ways that have hurt others and harmed ourselves – and for our negligence – the times when we fail to speak out, or to do the loving thing required of us. In acknowledging the reality of sin in our lives, in society and in our world, we open ourselves to receive God's gift of forgiveness, and express our intention to make a new beginning.

4.5 'Most merciful God...'

Most merciful God,
Father of our Lord Jesus Christ,
we confess that we have sinned
in thought, word and deed.
We have not loved you with our whole heart.
We have not loved our neighbours as ourselves.
In your mercy
forgive what we have been,
help us to amend what we are,
and direct what we shall be;
that we may do justly,
love mercy,
and walk humbly with you, our God. Amen.

In this prayer, sin is spelt out in relation to the Summary of the Law (4.2 above): it is our failure to love God and our neighbour in what we think, say and do. The prayer is clear that we depend upon God's grace to be and do what God calls us to be and do. In asking for God's mercy and forgiveness, we not only acknowledge our wrongdoing, but express our intention to live better lives directed by the will of God.

This alternative modern-language prayer of Confession originated as a Presbyterian prayer, which found its way into the **Joint Liturgical Group**'s *Daily Prayer* (1968). From there, it came to be included in the Church of England's services of Morning and Evening Prayer (Series 2). It was first incorporated (in an adapted form) into an Anglican Eucharist in the 1985 Prayer Book of the Anglican Church of Canada. In *Common Worship*, the prayer has been adapted to end with a direct quotation of Micah 6.8.

4.6 'Almighty God, Father of our Lord Jesus Christ...'

Almighty God,
Father of our Lord Jesus Christ,
Maker of all things, Judge of all men:
we acknowledge and bewail
our manifold sins and wickedness,
which we from time to time

most grievously have committed,
by thought, word, and deed,
against thy Divine Majesty,
provoking most justly thy wrath and indignation against us.
We do earnestly repent,
and are heartily sorry for these our misdoings;
the remembrance of them is grievous unto us;
the burden of them is intolerable.
Have mercy upon us,
have mercy upon us, most merciful Father;
for thy Son our Lord Jesus Christ's sake,
forgive us all that is past;
and grant that we may ever hereafter
serve and please thee in newness of life,
to the honour and glory of thy Name;
through Jesus Christ our Lord. Amen.

This is the prayer for the confession of sins at the Holy Communion service in the *Book of Common Prayer*. Cranmer believed that those who received Communion needed to prepare themselves carefully to take their place around the table of the Lord. His prayer deliberately reminds us that we come before a God who is our Judge as well as our Saviour. At the same time, Cranmer was careful to place the prayer after a long Exhortation (very seldom used today, even in churches that cherish the Prayer Book), which emphasizes the infinite mercy of God, and the comfort that a Christian should take in that mercy. The layering of language in this confession conveys a sense of how sin accumulates, and impedes our progress in the Christian way. The burden of past sins is finally resolved in the confidence that a new beginning is possible. We know from our own experience that people can feel burdened by the memory of past wrongs, and there are likely to be moments in life when we need to be freed from a crippling sense of the past, and to recover our sense of the overflowing mercy of God.

4.7 'Almighty and most merciful Father...'

Almighty and most merciful Father,
we have erred and strayed from thy ways like lost sheep,
we have followed too much the devices and desires of our own hearts,

we have offended against thy holy laws,
we have left undone those things which we ought to have done,
and we have done those things which we ought not to have done;
and there is no health in us.
But thou, O Lord, have mercy upon us, miserable offenders.
Spare thou them, O God, which confess their faults,
restore thou them that are penitent,
according to thy promise declared unto mankind
in Christ Jesu our Lord.
And grant, O most merciful Father, for his sake,
that we may hereafter live a godly, righteous, and sober life,
to the glory of thy holy Name. Amen.

One of Cranmer's greatest achievements was to combine the seven medieval monastic daily services into two relatively simple forms of daily worship, Morning Prayer and Evening Prayer, which were to be said in English by priests and people together in every church and chapel in the land. Cranmer prefaced this prayer of corporate confession to the services of Morning Prayer and Evening Prayer in the **1552 Prayer Book**. Its multiplication of metaphors, of straying, offending, and there being no health in us, extends our understanding of sin beyond simply wrongdoing.

We know that we can be headstrong in seeking to go our own way, apart from God, until we arrive at a place where there is no way to go forward at all. But in turning again to God at that point, we are given the grace that can enable the rest of our life to 'be pure and holy', and a preparation for 'eternal joy'.

4.8 The Prayer of Humble Access

We do not presume
to come to this your table, merciful Lord,
trusting in our own righteousness,
but in your manifold and great mercies.
We are not worthy
so much as to gather up the crumbs under your table.
But you are the same Lord
whose nature is always to have mercy.
Grant us therefore, gracious Lord,
so to eat the flesh of your dear Son Jesus Christ

and to drink his blood,
that our sinful bodies may be made clean by his body
and our souls washed through his most precious blood,
and that we may evermore dwell in him, and he in us. Amen.

We do not presume
to come to this thy Table, O merciful Lord,
trusting in our own righteousness,
but in thy manifold and great mercies.
We are not worthy
so much as to gather up the crumbs from under thy Table.
But thou art the same Lord,
whose property is always to have mercy.
Grant us therefore, gracious Lord,
so to eat the flesh of thy dear Son
Jesus Christ,
and to drink his blood,
that our sinful bodies may be made clean by his body,
and our souls washed through his most precious blood,
and that we may evermore dwell in him,
and he in us. Amen.

Anglicans are wary of defining too closely what happens at the Eucharist, but caution is very far from indifference. Holy Communion is to be taken seriously: Cranmer used the expression 'holy mysteries' when referring to the bread and wine of communion. Saint Paul spoke of the need to discern the body (1 Corinthians 11.27–29), and early Christian writers insisted that what is received in communion is no ordinary food and drink. What Christ promises us, he will give, even if we cannot say exactly how this happens. He comes not simply to meet us, but to dwell in us, as he and the Father dwell in one another. We receive the tokens of his abiding love, for which we have to prepare as we approach the holy table.

This prayer was composed by Cranmer, and placed immediately before the administration of Communion in the **1549 Prayer Book**. It alludes directly to the story of the encounter between Jesus and the Syro-Phoenecian woman (Mark 7.24–30): like her, we should approach the holy table with humble but firm determination, unworthy as we are. In the **1552 Prayer Book**, the prayer was moved to a position between the *Sanctus* and the **institution narrative**, and it stayed in that place in 1662. A modern English version is provided in

Common Worship (Order One), as an optional prayer in the original position, immediately before the sharing of Communion.

4.9 'Almighty God, we thank you for feeding us...'

Almighty God,
we thank you for feeding us
with the body and blood of your Son Jesus Christ.
Through him we offer you our souls and bodies
to be a living sacrifice.
Send us out in the power of your Spirit
to live and work
to your praise and glory. Amen.

Almighty God,
we thank thee for feeding us
with the body and blood of thy Son Jesus Christ.
Through him we offer thee our souls and bodies to be a living sacrifice.
Send us out in the power of thy Spirit
to live and work
to thy praise and glory. Amen.

From Common Worship

This is (with 4.10) one of two prayers written in the 1970s, to be said after the people have received communion. It became familiar through its inclusion in the 1980 *Alternative Service Book*. Both prayers continue in use in *Common Worship*.

The prayer begins with a note of praise, expressed as self-offering, and moves to articulate a sense of mission – 'send us out in the power of your/ thy Spirit'. It echoes a prayer in the *Book of Common Prayer*: 'here we offer and present unto thee, O Lord, ourselves, our souls and bodies, to be a reasonable, holy and lively sacrifice unto thee', said by the minister after the giving of Holy Communion.

There are two vital movements in the Eucharist. We are gathered together to be the body of Christ in a particular time and place (cf. 1 Corinthians 10.16–17), and we are sent out to bear witness to Christ in all that we are and say and do. St Paul speaks of us offering our bodies – all our living, in its everyday circumstances – as a spiritual sacrifice and an act of worship (Romans

12.1). But how can we offer anything to God? The offering of our bodies to God is only possible in so far as we have been joined through communion to Christ, the Lord who offered himself in perfect love and obedience to the Father.

4.10 *'Father of all, we give you thanks and praise...'*

Father of all,
we give you thanks and praise,
that when we were still far off
you met us in your Son and brought us home.
Dying and living, he declared your love,
gave us grace, and opened the gate of glory.
May we who share Christ's body live his risen life;
we who drink his cup bring life to others;
we whom the Spirit lights give light to the world.
Keep us firm in the hope you have set before us,
so we and all your children shall be free,
and the whole earth live to praise your name;
through Christ our Lord.
Amen.

This prayer first appeared in the modern English-language service **Series 3,** as an alternative to the Prayer of Humble Access [4.8], to be said by 'one of the ministers' alone. It was incorporated into the *Alternative Service Book*, through which it entered into the affection of Anglican worshippers. It is retained in *Common Worship* (Order One), as a prayer that all may say together after receiving communion. It expresses, in a rich tapestry of New Testament imagery and allusion, the story of Christian salvation. In communion, God goes out to meet us in Christ, as the loving father went out to meet his prodigal son. We then ask that, through our sharing in Christ's life, we may bear him in our lives, be held firm in the hope of the liberty of the children of God, and add our voices to all creation's hymn of praise (cf. Hebrews 6.19, Romans 8, Revelation 5.13).

4.11 Gloria in excelsis

Glory to God in the highest,
and peace to his people on earth.

Lord God, heavenly King,
almighty God and Father,
we worship you, we give you thanks,
we praise you for your glory.

Lord Jesus Christ, only Son of the Father,
Lord God, Lamb of God,
you take away the sin of the world:
have mercy on us;
you are seated at the right hand of the Father:
receive our prayer.

For you alone are the Holy One,
you alone are the Lord,
you alone are the Most High, Jesus Christ,
with the Holy Spirit,
in the glory of God the Father.
Amen.

Glory be to God on high,
and in earth peace, goodwill towards men.
We praise thee, we bless thee,
we worship thee, we glorify thee,
we give thanks to thee for thy great glory,
O Lord God, heavenly King,
God the Father Almighty.
O Lord, the only-begotten Son, Jesu Christ;
O Lord God, Lamb of God, Son of the Father,
that takest away the sins of the world,
have mercy upon us.
Thou that takest away the sins of the world,
have mercy upon us.
Thou that takest away the sins of the world,
receive our prayer.

Words for Worship

Thou that sittest at the right hand of God the Father,
have mercy upon us.
For thou only art holy;
thou only art the Lord;
thou only, O Christ, with the Holy Ghost,
art most high in the glory of God the Father.
Amen.

The opening line of this model 'worship song' echoes the song of the angels at Christ's birth (Luke 2.14). The verbs 'we worship you, we give you thanks, we praise you' remind us precisely what worship is, and in it we join our voices to the whole company of heaven. With John the Baptist, we recognize 'the Lamb of God, that takes away the sins of the world' (John 1.29), and we join the saints as they sing their song of glory before the throne of the Lamb (Revelation 4.11).

Gloria in excelsis began as a **canticle** for Morning Prayer in the eastern Christian tradition. In the sixth century it was adopted into the Mass in the **Roman rite**, as an opening hymn. Cranmer kept the Gloria in the traditional position in the **1549 Prayer Book**, but in 1552 he placed it just before the final blessing at the end of the service, so that the whole act of worship ends on a note of praise. In *Common Worship*, the *Gloria* may be used either in its original position before the collect (in Order One), or in the position directed by Cranmer (in Order Two). It is traditional not to use the Gloria during the seasons of **Advent** or **Lent**, in keeping with the more simplified mood of these times of preparation for the great feasts of Christmas and Easter.

5

The Nicene Creed

We believe in one God,
the Father, the Almighty,
maker of heaven and earth,
of all that is,
seen and unseen.

We believe in one Lord, Jesus Christ,
the only Son of God,
eternally begotten of the Father,
God from God, Light from Light,
true God from true God,
begotten, not made,
of one Being with the Father;
through him all things were made.
For us and for our salvation he came down from heaven,
was incarnate from the Holy Spirit and the Virgin Mary
and was made man.
For our sake he was crucified under Pontius Pilate;
he suffered death and was buried.
On the third day he rose again
in accordance with the Scriptures;
he ascended into heaven
and is seated at the right hand of the Father.
He will come again in glory to judge the living and the dead,
and his kingdom will have no end.

We believe in the Holy Spirit,
the Lord, the giver of life,
who proceeds from the Father and the Son,
who with the Father and the Son is worshipped and glorified,
who has spoken through the prophets.
We believe in one holy catholic and apostolic Church.
We acknowledge one baptism for the forgiveness of sins.
We look for the resurrection of the dead,
and the life of the world to come.
Amen.

I believe in one God the Father Almighty,
maker of heaven and earth,
and of all things
visible and invisible:

And in one Lord Jesus Christ,
the only-begotten Son of God,
begotten of his Father before all worlds,
God of God, Light of Light,
very God of very God,
begotten, not made,
being of one substance with the Father,
by whom all things were made:
who for us men and for our salvation
came down from heaven,
and was incarnate by the Holy Ghost of the Virgin Mary,
and was made man,
and was crucified also for us under Pontius Pilate.
He suffered and was buried,
and the third day he rose again
according to the Scriptures,
and ascended into heaven,
and sitteth on the right hand of the Father.

And he shall come again with glory
to judge both the quick and the dead:
whose kingdom shall have no end.

And I believe in the Holy Ghost,
the Lord and giver of life,
who proceedeth from the Father and the Son,
who with the Father and the Son together
is worshipped and glorified,
who spake by the prophets.
And I believe one Catholick and Apostolick Church.
I acknowledge one baptism for the remission of sins.
And I look for the Resurrection of the dead,
and the life of the world to come. Amen.

This summary of Christian belief is most usually recited by the congregation together during the Eucharist, immediately after and as a response to the proclamation of the Word in the reading and sermon. Because it is a statement of what Christians believe collectively, it originally began with the words 'We believe', and modern-language services have returned to this form (as in *Common Worship* Order One). The singular 'I believe', which turns the Creed into a statement of individual faith, may have come about from the use of this text at baptisms. It became widespread in the Middle Ages, and was continued in the *Book of Common Prayer*.

The Creed is divided into four sections: a statement about God the Father, a second about the Son, a third about the Holy Spirit, and a fourth (much shorter one) about the Church and the future. The shape and contents reflect the vigorous controversies about Christian belief that shook the Church in the fourth century. Indeed, the Creed is traditionally called 'The Nicene Creed' after the Council of Nicaea in 325 AD, at which the eternal relation of the Son to the Father was the central question. The text reached almost its present form at a later meeting of bishops, the Council of Constantinople in 381, by which time the place of the Holy Spirit within the Trinity had also been much discussed. The central concern of the Nicene Creed is therefore with the relationship of the three Persons of the Trinity to one another, though it also has much to say about their relation to the world in creation, redemption, judgement and inspiration. The incarnate Christ is presented as complete in his humanity (of his human mother, already named with the traditional title 'the Virgin Mary') and complete in his divinity (of the Holy Spirit).

Words for Worship

The Nicene Creed has continued in use for centuries with little change. One alteration, though, has had a great effect in Christian history, and is the source of controversy within the Church to this day. In the western churches, it has been usual from about the ninth century to say that the Spirit proceeds 'from the Father and the Son'; in the original version of 381, still in use in the eastern churches, the Spirit proceeds 'from the Father'. The western addition is usually called the *Filioque*. The argument is both about whether the addition is true, and whether the western church had the right to alter a shared text unilaterally. In *Common Worship*, an alternative text of the Nicene Creed without the *Filioque* is made available, for use 'on suitable ecumenical occasions'.

6

Gospel Canticles

A Canticle is a song of praise. St Luke's account, in the opening chapters of his Gospel, of the conception and birth of John the Baptist and of Jesus, is punctuated with such songs, sung by central characters in the story. These are commonly known as the 'Gospel Canticles'.

6.1 Benedictus (The Song of Zechariah)

Blessed be the Lord the God of Israel,
who has come to his people and set them free.
He has raised up for us a mighty Saviour,
born of the house of his servant David.
Through his holy prophets God promised of old
to save us from our enemies,
from the hands of all that hate us,
To show mercy to our ancestors,
and to remember his holy covenant.
This was the oath God swore to our father Abraham:
to set us free from the hands of our enemies.
Free to worship him without fear,
holy and righteous in his sight
all the days of our life.
And you, child, shall be called the prophet of the Most High,
for you will go before the Lord to prepare his way,
to give his people knowledge of salvation
by the forgiveness of all their sins.
In the tender compassion of our God
the dawn from on high shall break upon us,
to shine on those who dwell in darkness and the shadow of death,
and to guide our feet into the way of peace.

Blessed be the Lord God of Israel,
for he hath visited, and redeemed his people;
and hath raised up a mighty salvation for us,
in the house of his servant David.
As he spake by the mouth of his holy Prophets,
which have been since the world began;
that we should be saved from our enemies,
and from the hands of all that hate us;
to perform the mercy promised to our forefathers,
and to remember his holy covenant;
to perform the oath which he sware to our forefather Abraham,
that he would give us,
that we being delivered out of the hands of our enemies,
might serve him without fear,
in holiness and righteousness before him, all the days of our life.
And thou, child, shalt be called the Prophet of the Highest,
for thou shalt go before the face of the Lord to prepare his ways,
to give knowledge of salvation unto his people
for the remission of their sins;
through the tender mercy of our God
whereby the dayspring from on high hath visited us,
to give light to them that sit in darkness and the shadow of death,
and to guide our feet into the way of peace.

John the Baptist and Jesus were related to each other: 'cousins' in the wide sense of the word that is still used in the Middle East today. After the Baptist's birth, when his father Zechariah agrees that the boy may be named John, Zechariah miraculously recovers the power of speech and sings this canticle (Luke 1.68–79), known as the *Benedictus* from its opening word in Latin. The reference to the breaking of a new dawn ('the dayspring from on high') makes this an especially appropriate biblical passage to recite at Morning Prayer, and it has been used in this way since the sixth century: we welcome the promise of a new day in Christ, as Zechariah welcomed a new beginning from God.

6.2 Magnificat (The Song of Mary)

My soul proclaims the greatness of the Lord,
my spirit rejoices in God my Saviour;
he has looked with favour on his lowly servant.
From this day all generations will call me blessed;
the Almighty has done great things for me and holy is his name.
He has mercy on those who fear him,
from generation to generation.
He has shown strength with his arm,
and has scattered the proud in their conceit,
casting down the mighty from their thrones
and lifting up the lowly.
He has filled the hungry with good things
and sent the rich away empty.
He has come to the aid of his servant Israel,
to remember his promise of mercy,
the promise made to our ancestors,
to Abraham and his children for ever.

My soul doth magnify the Lord,
and my spirit hath rejoiced in God my Saviour;
for he hath regarded the lowliness of his hand-maiden.
For behold, from henceforth all generations shall call me blessed;
for he that is mighty hath magnified me, and holy is his Name.
And his mercy is on them that fear him,
throughout all generations.
He hath shewed strength with his arm,
he hath scattered the proud in the imagination of their hearts.
He hath put down the mighty from their seat,
and hath exalted the humble and meek.
He hath filled the hungry with good things,
and the rich he hath sent empty away.
He remembering his mercy
hath holpen his servant Israel,
as he promised to our forefathers,
Abraham and his seed for ever.

Luke's Gospel describes (1.39–45) how Mary, carrying the unborn Jesus, went to visit her kinswoman Elizabeth, pregnant with John the Baptist. Elizabeth pronounces that Mary is blessed, and Mary responds with this song (1.46–55), known as the *Magnificat* from its opening word in Latin. The true glory is given by Mary to God, in a song deeply coloured by Old Testament tradition (there are specially close echoes of the Song of Hannah, Samuel's mother [1 Samuel 2.1–10]). In the incarnation of Jesus, worldly values are turned upside down, and God inaugurates the new and revolutionary state of things that is his kingdom. In the medieval Church, the Magnificat was regularly sung at the evening service of **vespers**. When, in the **1549 Prayer Book**, Cranmer brought together elements of vespers and **compline** to form the service of Evening Prayer, the Magnificat found its traditional Anglican place as the canticle following the first reading.

6.3 Nunc Dimittis (The Song of Simeon)

Now, Lord, you let your servant go in peace:
your word has been fulfilled.
My own eyes have seen the salvation
which you have prepared in the sight of every people;
a light to reveal you to the nations
and the glory of your people Israel.

Lord, now lettest thou thy servant depart in peace:
according to thy word.
For mine eyes have seen thy salvation;
which thou hast prepared before the face of all people;
to be a light to lighten the Gentiles:
and to be the glory of thy people Israel.

These words are used most often during evening acts of worship, and at funeral services. They are from St Luke's Gospel (Luke 2.29–32), where they are spoken in the Temple in Jerusalem by Simeon, a devout and righteous man who has been promised that before his death, he will see the Lord's Messiah. When the infant Jesus is brought to the Temple by his parents to be presented to the Lord, Simeon greets them and takes the child in his arms as he says these words, praising God for a gift that will bring glory to his ancient people, and will be a revelation to those who do not yet know him. At the

25

same time, Simeon acknowledges the reality of his own forthcoming death. In the medieval west, the *Nunc Dimittis* was sung at the late evening service of **compline**. Cranmer incorporated it from there into his service of Evening Prayer, placing it after the second reading.

Used in worship, the words remind Christian people that while our life on this earth will inevitably draw to a close, we are assured of salvation through the coming of Jesus, and we can live and leave in peace. The song is commonly known by its opening words in Latin translation: *Nunc dimittis*, that is 'Now you send' or 'Now you let go' your servant in peace.

7

Prayers from the *Book of Common Prayer*

7.1 A Prayer of St Chrysostom

Almighty God,
who hast given us grace at this time with one accord
to make our common supplications unto thee;
and dost promise that when two or three are gathered together
in thy Name
thou wilt grant their requests:
Fulfil now, O Lord, the desires and petitions of thy servants,
as may be most expedient for them;
granting us in this world knowledge of thy truth,
and in the world to come life everlasting. Amen.

This prayer opens with a clear statement that our prayer for others is always God's work in us, and reiterates Christ's promised presence when two or three gather together in his name (Matthew 18:20). We do not only express our desires and petitions in prayer, but find that in the very act of praying, our wants and needs are unravelled. For true prayer is prayer aligned to the will of God, and our growing in the Spirit requires us to see that what we want, for ourselves as much as for others, is not always what we actually need.

Although the prayer is attributed to St John Chrysostom (archbishop of Constantinople from 398 to 404), it is almost certainly a product of later Greek liturgy. It was first adopted by Cranmer in 1544 for a Litany that was his earliest liturgical project of casting public prayer in the English language. The prayer was later used as the final prayer for Morning and Evening Prayer in the **1662 Prayer Book**, just before the concluding Grace.

7.2 A Prayer for all Conditions of men

O God, the Creator and Preserver of all mankind,
we humbly beseech thee for all sorts and conditions of men;
that thou wouldest be pleased to make thy ways known unto them,
thy saving health unto all nations.
More especially we pray thee for the good estate of the Catholick Church;
that it may be so guided and governed by thy good Spirit,
that all who profess and call themselves Christians
may be led into the way of truth,
and hold the faith in unity of Spirit,
in the bond of peace, and in righteousness of life.
Finally we commend to thy fatherly goodness all those,
who are in any ways afflicted or distressed in mind, body, or estate;
[*especially those for whom our prayers are desired;*]
that it may please thee to comfort and relieve them,
according to their several necessities,
giving them patience under their sufferings,
and a happy issue out of all their afflictions.
And this we beg for Jesus Christ his sake. Amen.

This general **intercession** first appeared in the **1662 Prayer Book**, for use on occasions when the **Litany** is not used.

No one is certain who wrote it, and there are grounds for thinking that it may be a shortened form of a longer original. It brilliantly manages to pray for a wide range of people in a very few words. The prayer divides into three sections: a **petition** for all human beings, a petition for the 'Catholick' (i.e. universal) Church, and petition for those in any kind of need. Some of its phrases, such as 'all sorts and conditions of men' and 'a happy issue out of all their afflictions', have become familiar phrases in the English language. The prayer helpfully allows the particular requests of the congregation to be inserted within the set form of words.

7.3 The General Thanksgiving

Almighty God, Father of all mercies,
we thine unworthy servants do give thee most humble and hearty thanks
for all thy goodness and loving-kindness to us and to all men;
[*particularly to those who desire now to offer up their praises and thanksgiving for thy late
merits vouchsafed unto them.*]
We bless thee for our creation, preservation,
and all the blessings of this life;
but above all for thine inestimable love
in the redemption of the world by our Lord Jesus Christ,
for the means of grace, and for the hope of glory.
And we beseech thee, give us that due sense of all thy mercies,
that our hearts may be unfeignedly thankful,
and that we show forth thy praise,
not only with our lips, but in our lives;
by giving up ourselves to thy service,
and walking before thee in holiness and righteousness all our days;
through Jesus Christ our Lord,
to whom with thee and the Holy Ghost
be all honour and glory, world without end. Amen.

This prayer first appeared in the **1662 Prayer Book**. It was written by Edward
Reynolds, who was Bishop of Norwich between 1661 and 1676.

It appears in a section entitled 'Prayers and Thanksgivings', and may
be used on any appropriate occasion in public or private prayer. The prayer
encompasses, within a relatively brief text, the fundamental basis of prayer in a
sense of thanksgiving for God's gifts to us in both creation and redemption – a
'due sense of all thy mercies' – with an eloquent human response in gratitude,
praise, self-offering and commitment to walk in holiness of life. An optional
clause is included as a thank-offering for particular mercies.

It is not surprising that this is a prayer earlier generations of children were
made to learn by heart. While we may not now impose learning it by rote, to
pray it frequently is to write it in our hearts, so that in time we are able to pray
it as we breathe.

7.4 Veni Creator

Come, Holy Ghost, our souls inspire,
And lighten with celestial fire;
Thou the anointing Spirit art,
Who dost thy sev'nfold gifts impart.

Thy blessed Unction from above
Is comfort, life, and fire of love;
Enable with perpetual light
The dullness of our blinded sight.

Anoint and cheer our soiled face
With the abundance of thy grace;
Keep far our foes, give peace at home;
Where thou art Guide, no ill can come.

Teach us to know the Father, Son,
And thee, of both, to be but One;
That through the ages all along
This, may be our endless song.
  Praise to thy eternal merit,
  Father, Son, and Holy Spirit.

This translation of a ninth-century Latin hymn was made by John Cosin, Bishop of Durham from 1660 to 1672. It was included in the **1662 Prayer Book**, as one of two alternative translations, in the prayers at the ordinations of priests and bishops. The *Veni Creator* is still used at ordinations today, usually in Cosin's translation. The reference to the seven-fold gifts of the Spirit alludes primarily to Isaiah 11.2–3 ('the spirit of wisdom and understanding, the spirit of counsel and might, the spirit of knowledge and the fear of the Lord'), but also echoes the medieval tradition of seven sacraments. It is among the most expressive evocations of the Holy Spirit, and is often reprinted in modern hymn books.

8

Classic collects

A collect is a short prayer that encompasses (or 'collects') the prayers of the worshipping community – as it gathers together to celebrate the Eucharist, or gathers together its petitions towards the end of Morning and Evening Prayer.

8.1 A morning collect

O Lord, our heavenly Father,
Almighty and everlasting God,
who hast safely brought us to the beginning of this day:
Defend us in the same with thy mighty power;
and grant that this day we fall into no sin,
neither run into any kind of danger;
but that all our doings may be ordered by thy governance,
to do always that is righteous in thy sight;
through Jesus Christ our Lord. Amen.

The **1549 Prayer Book** makes this the concluding collect at Morning Prayer, with the title 'for Grace'. While the word 'grace' does not appear in the text, the collect is a profound expression of our dependence on God's gracious protection. God is the one who brings us safely through sleep and darkness, so we pray that God's providential grace will guide and keep us during the day.

Cranmer drew this collect, which is based on a prayer in the Gelasian and Gregorian **sacramentaries**, from the medieval Sarum **Breviary**. It was used there at the first office of the day, said as dawn was breaking.

8.2 An evening collect

Lighten our darkness, we beseech thee, O Lord;
and by thy great mercy defend us
from all perils and dangers of this night;
for the love of thy only Son, our Saviour, Jesus Christ. Amen.

This is the concluding collect at Evening Prayer in the *Book of Common Prayer*, entitled 'for Aid against all Perils'. Its simplicity as a plea for light as darkness descends, and for defence against the perils of the night, has made it a greatly loved prayer of the Anglican tradition. 'Our darkness' may be interpreted as a reference to nightfall, but also to spiritual darkness, in our struggle against the darkness of sin and evil.

Cranmer drew this collect, which is based on a prayer in the Gelasian and Gregorian **sacramentaries**, from the medieval Sarum **Breviary**. It was used there at the office of **compline**, at the close of the day. In *Common Worship: Daily Prayer* this collect is used at Evening Prayer on Sundays.

8.3 The Collect of Advent Sunday

Almighty God, give us grace
that we may cast away the works of darkness,
and put upon us the armour of light,
now in the time of this mortal life,
in which thy Son Jesus Christ came to visit us in great humility;
that in the last day,
when he shall come in his glorious Majesty
to judge both the quick and the dead,
we may rise to the life immortal,
through him who liveth and reigneth
with thee and the Holy Ghost, now and for ever. Amen.

This prayer is appointed as the Collect of Advent Sunday in the *Book of Common Prayer* and in *Common Worship*, but is also used as a seasonal collect throughout the Advent season.

Advent invites us to prepare both for Christ's first coming at Christmas and for his second coming at the end of time, and these emphases are skilfully incorporated in the prayer. It contrasts Christ's first coming 'in great humility' with his second 'in ... glorious Majesty'. But Christ also comes to us 'now in the time of this mortal life', to rouse us to active discipleship today.

The collect was written for the **1549 Prayer Book**. It draws on the Epistle and Gospel set for Advent Sunday, on Romans 13 (with its imagery of the armour of light), and on the 'great humility' of Jesus' incarnation.

8.4 The Collect of the Second Sunday of Advent

Blessed Lord,
who hast caused all holy Scriptures to be written for our learning:
Grant that we may in such wise hear them,
read, mark, learn, and inwardly digest them,
that by patience and comfort of thy holy Word,
we may embrace and ever hold fast
the blessed hope of everlasting life,
which thou hast given us in our Saviour Jesus Christ. Amen.

This collect was composed by Cranmer for the **1549 Prayer Book**. It perfectly expresses the insistence of the English reformers that people should know and cherish their Scriptures, now made available to them in their own language, an insistence that has continued to characterize the Church of England in every generation. Notice that we pray first that we may *hear* the Scriptures. They are the proclamation of God's word, and they are to be *heard* with the ears before they are *read* with the eyes. In *Common Worship*, a version of this prayer in modern dress becomes the Collect for Bible Sunday, the Last Sunday after Trinity.

8.5 The Collect of Christmas Day

Almighty God,
who hast given us thy only-begotten Son
to take our nature upon him,
and as at this time to be born of a pure Virgin:
Grant that we being regenerate,
and made thy children by adoption and grace,
may daily be renewed by thy Holy Spirit;
through the same our Lord Jesus Christ,
who liveth and reigneth with thee and the same Spirit,
ever one God, world without end. Amen.

With great economy of words, this collect expresses the fundamental truths of the incarnation. The eternal Son of God takes upon himself our human nature and is born of the Virgin Mary his mother. In response, we pray that we may be regenerate, or born again, and live daily in the power of the Holy Spirit.

This collect was adapted from the Gelasian and Gregorian **sacramentaries** for the Eucharist during the day on Christmas Day. In the *Book of Common Prayer* it is appointed both for Christmas Day, and for the seven days following; the Epistle for the Sunday after Christmas Day (Galatians 4) also takes up the theme of 'adoption'. In *Common Worship* the collect is used at any daytime Christmas Eucharist.

8.6 The Collect of Ash Wednesday

Almighty and everlasting God,
who hatest nothing that thou hast made,
and dost forgive the sins of all them that are penitent:
Create and make in us new and contrite hearts,
that we worthily lamenting our sins,
and acknowledging our wretchedness,
may obtain of thee, the God of all mercy,
perfect remission and forgiveness;
through Jesus Christ our Lord. Amen.

This collect sets the tone for Ash Wednesday as a special day of repentance and fasting, and for the whole season of Lent as a time of penitence and preparation for Easter. In the *Book of Common Prayer*, it is used every day throughout Lent, and *Common Worship* allows it to be used in this way also. The language of the collect is drawn from the Book of Wisdom, in the **Apocrypha** (Wisdom 11.23–24), and from Psalm 51.10. God alone, abundant in mercy, is able to renew our sinful human nature.

This prayer was composed for the **1549 Prayer Book**.

8.7 The Collect of Easter Day

Almighty God,
who through thine only-begotten Son Jesus Christ
hast overcome death,
and opened unto us the gate of everlasting life:
We humbly beseech thee,
that as by thy special grace preventing us
thou dost put into our minds good desires,

so by thy continual help we may bring the same to good effect;
through Jesus Christ our Lord,
who liveth and reigneth with thee and the Holy Ghost,
ever one God, world without end. Amen.

The joyful news of Easter is not only that God in Christ has conquered death, but that we too have a share in Christ's resurrection: in him a gate has been opened for us. The Resurrection was God's loving initiative, and this prayer goes on to ask that this sustaining grace, which implants good desires into our hearts, may issue in active and godly discipleship. 'Prevent' in older sixteenth century English means 'go before' (from Latin *praevenio*), rather than 'stop' or 'inhibit'. The initiative is always God's.

8.8 The Collect of Whitsunday

God, who as at this time didst teach the hearts of thy faithful people,
by the sending to them the light of thy Holy Spirit:
Grant us by the same Spirit to have a right judgement in all things,
and evermore to rejoice in his holy comfort;
through the merits of Christ Jesus our Saviour,
who liveth and reigneth with thee,
in the unity of the same Spirit,
one God, world without end. Amen.

Whitsunday, or Pentecost, celebrates the outpouring of the Holy Spirit on the Church in fulfilment of Jesus' promise (Acts 2), 50 days after his resurrection (hence the name 'Pentecost', which derives from the Greek word for 50). The Spirit teaches us, enlightens us, gives us wisdom in discernment and decision-making, and brings 'comfort', a word that also embraces ideas of inward strength and counsel. Pentecost was considered an especially suitable day for baptism, next after only Easter itself, and the popular name of 'Whitsunday' is thought to come from the white robes worn by the newly baptized. In fact, the normal liturgical colour for this day is red.

8.9 The Collect of All Saints' Day

O Almighty God,
who hast knit together thine elect in one communion and fellowship,
in the mystical body of thy Son Christ our Lord:

Grant us grace so to follow thy blessed Saints
in all virtuous and godly living,
that we may come to those unspeakable joys,
which thou hast prepared for them that unfeignedly love thee;
through Jesus Christ our Lord. Amen.

The Feast of All Saints is celebrated on 1 November (in *Common Worship*, it may be celebrated on the nearest Sunday). It celebrates the great heroes and heroines of the Faith, as well as countless thousands who have served God in their earthly lives and are now at rest. Drawing on St Paul's teaching that the Church is 'the body of Christ', the collect emphasizes the continuing unity of saints below and above, joined together in the mystical or spiritual body of Christ. It asks that, following the example of the saints 'in all virtuous and godly living', we also may attain the fullness of joy. This collect was written for the **1549 Prayer Book**.

8.10 The Collect of the Fourth Sunday after Trinity

O God, the protector of all that trust in thee,
without whom nothing is strong, nothing is holy:
Increase and multiply upon us thy mercy;
that, thou being our ruler and guide,
we may so pass through things temporal,
that we finally lose not the things eternal:
Grant this, O heavenly Father, for Jesus Christ's sake our Lord.
Amen.

Notice in this collect the attributes of God: our protector, ruler and guide; the source of strength, holiness and mercy. The collect places our lives under divine providence, asking that we have such a grasp of all God's mercies, that we live our earthly life ('things temporal') in such a way as not finally to lose eternal life.

This prayer was adapted from the Gregorian **sacramentary** for the **1549 Prayer Book**.

8.11 The Collect of the Nineteenth Sunday after Trinity

O God, forasmuch as without thee
we are not able to please thee;
Mercifully grant that thy Holy Spirit may in all things
direct and rule our hearts;
through Jesus Christ our Lord. Amen.

The strength of this collect lies in its simplicity. Without God's mercy and help we are unable to live lives pleasing to him. We ask that God's Holy Spirit may be the Lord of our hearts. This is a succinct prayer for God's guidance and help, both generally and in relation to specific purposes or occasions.

9

Modern collects for various seasons

9.1 Advent

Almighty God,
purify our hearts and minds,
that when your Son Jesus Christ comes again as judge and saviour
we may be ready to receive him,
who is our Lord and our God.

This collect has its roots in a prayer that was traditionally said before the celebration of Holy Communion, and reshapes it in the light of the central Advent theme of judgement. At Advent, we look forward to the coming (*adventus*) of Christ as judge. Here we pray, in language of great simplicity, that God will himself purify both our feelings and affections (our 'hearts') and our capacity for understanding (our 'minds'), so that we may be ready to sustain this tremendous event.

9.2 Christmas Night

Eternal God,
in the stillness of this night
you sent your almighty Word
to pierce the world's darkness with the light of salvation:
give to the earth the peace that we long for
and fill our hearts with the joy of heaven
through our Saviour, Jesus Christ.

Two images are powerfully combined in the opening of this prayer. One is straight from Scripture: the Word as 'the light that shines in the darkness, and the darkness did not overcome it'. (John 1.5). The other, the Word of God as an utterance that breaks the surrounding silence, 'the Word going out from the silence of the Father', is found in many early Christian writers. A word spoken into silence, a light lit in the darkness, may be as tiny as this newborn child, but it makes everything utterly different. Now the peace that Isaiah foretells (Isaiah 11.6–9) becomes possible; now the shepherds' ears can hear (and human hearts experience) the song of the angels (Luke 2.13–14).

9.3 The Presentation of Christ in the Temple

Lord Jesus Christ,
light of the nations and glory of Israel:
make your home among us,
and present us pure and holy
to your heavenly Father,
your God, and our God.

Luke describes (2.22–38) how Mary and Joseph took Jesus to the Temple in Jerusalem when he was 40 days old, to present him to the Lord and to offer a sacrifice. This was done to fulfil a biblical command, that firstborn male children should be designated to the Lord (cf. Exodus 13.2). While at the Temple, they encounter two elderly prophets, Simeon and Anna. This collect picks up Simeon's description of Jesus as 'a light to lighten the nations' and 'the glory of your people Israel' (cf. The Song of Simeon, or *Nunc Dimittis*, at 6.3 above). As we gather in church on the Feast of the Presentation to remember how the infant Jesus was presented to the Lord God of Israel, we pray that Jesus himself, our Lord and Christ, will present us to his heavenly Father: and we imply that we can only be presented to the Father when we allow ourselves to be carried by Jesus.

9.4 Ash Wednesday

Holy God,
our lives are laid open before you:
rescue us from the chaos of sin
and through the death of your Son
bring us healing and make us whole
in Jesus Christ our Lord.

The 40 days before Easter have from early times been observed as a time of fasting and reflection. Those who had been separated from the Church's fellowship through sin prepared to be received back into Church at Easter, and had to show penitence for past wrongdoing; those who were to be baptized into the Church at Easter prepared themselves by turning away from their past lives. Sin dislocates right relationships, and leads to confusion and chaos: people will sometimes say, 'My life was (or is) chaotic.' As we turn to Christ in the course of Lent, we rediscover integrity and coherence in our lives, and claim that new beginning that is made possible by Jesus' gift of himself for us on the cross.

9.5 Easter Day

God of glory,
by the raising of your Son
you have broken the chains of death and hell:
fill your Church with faith and hope;
for a new day has dawned
and the way to life stands open
in our Saviour Jesus Christ.

In the eastern orthodox churches, the **icon** of Christ's resurrection (his *Anastasis*) shows him rescuing humankind from death. He grasps Adam and Eve by the arm, and pulls them out from the underground cavern that represents death and separation. The gates of death's cave are shattered, and broken chains are in the foreground. This prayer summons up that powerful image, and carries us forward into language of newness, hope and possibility.

9.6 Trinity Sunday

Holy God,
faithful and unchanging:
enlarge our minds with the knowledge of your truth,
and draw us more deeply into the mystery of your love,
that we may truly worship you,
Father, Son and Holy Spirit,
one God, now and for ever.

The Christian doctrine of the Trinity is not so much a statement about God's relationship to the world, as a revelation of what God is in God's own self: an endless movement of self-giving love and communication, in which Father, Son and Holy Spirit are in perfect relationship, without beginning and without end. As we contemplate this movement – which we can only do if our mental and spiritual capacity is enlarged by grace – we will find ourselves drawn more deeply into the movement of God's love itself. On this particular Sunday, we are reminded that the doctrine of the Trinity is no mere intellectual construction, though it challenges the mind immensely, but is an attempt to state the deepest of all truths: that God is not just loving, but God *is* love.

9.7 Sundays after Trinity

The Seventh Sunday after Trinity

Generous God,
you give us gifts and make them grow:
though our faith is as small as mustard seed,
make it grow to your glory
and the flourishing of your kingdom;
through Jesus Christ our Lord.

This collect draws on the imagery of growth in the natural world, in a way that Jesus often did in his own teaching. Its specific reference is to Jesus' saying: 'For truly I tell you, if you have faith the size of a mustard seed, you will say to this mountain, "Move from here to there", and it will move; and nothing will be impossible for you.' (Matthew 17.20). But the mention of the mustard seed puts us in mind also of the parable of the mustard seed, with its extraordinary capacity for growth (Matthew 13.31, Mark 4.31, Luke 13.19). Christian people pray for a faith that is creative and dynamic in the way that plant life grows, making the world an ever-growing and developing place.

The Thirteenth Sunday after Trinity

Almighty God,
you search us and know us:
may we rely on you in strength
and rest on you in weakness,
now and in all our days;
through Jesus Christ our Lord.

This collect takes its inspiration from Psalm 139.1: 'O Lord, you have searched me out and known me.' God, knowing us intimately and caring for us so deeply, seeks us out to support us when we are at our weakest; God equally encourages us with love in our times of strength and creativity.

The Twenty-First Sunday after Trinity

Almighty God,
in whose service lies perfect freedom:
teach us to obey you
with loving hearts and steadfast wills;
through Jesus Christ our Lord.

The Collect for Peace at Morning Prayer in the *Book of Common Prayer* provides the inspiration for the opening of this collect. It develops the idea of service by asking God to teach us to have loving hearts and steadfast wills, so that our service may indeed be generous and wholehearted.

9.8 Sundays before Advent

The Fourth Sunday before Advent

God of glory,
touch our lips with the fire of your Spirit,
that we with all creation
may rejoice to sing your praise;
through Jesus Christ our Lord.

Isaiah (6.1–8) describes an overwhelming experience of God in the Temple, at the end of which a seraph (literally, 'a burning one') touched his mouth with a burning coal, so that he could proclaim God's word to the nations. The fire of the coal both purifies, and sets speech on fire. So we too pray that our speech may be cleansed and purified, and that it may be set on fire: then we will be able to sing God's praise as it should be sung.

The Second Sunday before Advent

Heavenly Lord,
you long for the world's salvation:
stir us from apathy,
restrain us from excess
and revive in us new hope
that all creation will one day be healed
in Jesus Christ our Lord.

As the end of the liturgical year draws near, we pray for the healing of all creation, a healing for which God also yearns. As the autumn days grow darker, we are reminded of the revival of a new hope – and perhaps there is also a hint, in the mention of 'restraint from excess', of the impending season of Christmas merrymaking.

Where do words for our worship come from?

A brief history

The earliest Christian converts were Jews, and they would at first have continued to pray and worship in ways similar to those of some of their contemporaries; the chief difference was that their praise and thanksgiving were now being offered to 'the God and Father of our Lord Jesus Christ' (e.g. 1 Peter 1.3) and 'through Jesus Christ our Lord' (e.g. Romans 16.27). During the next century, as Gentiles came to outnumber Jews within the Christian movement, specifically Jewish characteristics in their worship gradually declined. Sunday came to replace the Sabbath as the weekly occasion for corporate worship (but not for rest); the Christian Eucharist replaced both the Sabbath evening meal and the weekly synagogue assembly; the annual celebration of Easter replaced the Passover; and baptism, derived from the practice of John the Baptist, became the universal rite of initiation into the Christian community.

To begin with, Christian gatherings would usually have been small in size and have taken place in private houses (and possibly workshops), but by the third century congregations were growing larger in some places, and even acquiring their own buildings. When in the fourth century Christians ceased to suffer persecution, purpose-built churches began to appear everywhere, and the larger size of most of these brought about changes in forms of worship. The services became more formalized, with an elevated style of ceremonial and language, and with processions and music. Because Christians were concerned that what was said in worship should be correct in doctrine, prayers were increasingly written down rather than extemporized or handed on orally, and local variations of practice gave way to a wider regional standardization. Many converts at this time had not always undergone a profound conversion experience, or absorbed fully the instruction that they had received, so the public rites stressed more strongly the majesty and transcendence of God, and the need for a sense of awe and of the sinfulness of humanity in his presence. This in turn led many Christians to feel unworthy to receive communion frequently, and for the services to be seen as something done by the clergy on behalf of the people, who increasingly understood themselves instead to be watching a sacred drama unfold before their eyes.

These tendencies grew as the centuries passed. The texts of the set prayers to be said by the president at a service were now gathered into a single book, known in the Latin-speaking west as a **sacramentary** (the Gelasian and Gregorian sacramentaries – named after popes who died in 496 and 604 respectively, though the sacramentaries themselves are somewhat later – are especially important as sources of prayers in the *Book of Common Prayer*). At the same time, the parts of the service to be said or sung by other ministers were gathered in other volumes, and the ceremonial directions were collected in yet another. Additions and revisions were made to these in the course of time and eventually, as it became common for there to be only one minister leading a service, the various texts were combined into a single book. That used by a priest for the Eucharist was known as a **missal**. In the eastern part of the ancient world, the major centres of Christianity developed patterns of worship that were related to one another but had their own distinctive features. In the western part, the **Roman rite** – originally merely the local practice of the city of Rome – eventually came to dominate other regional patterns, and to constitute the basis of all forms of worship there in the Middle Ages. The different rites belonging to the various dioceses in medieval England were just local variations of this Roman form; that of the diocese of Salisbury, known as the **Sarum rite**, was the one most widely adopted in the country. Except for a few words spoken by the couple in the marriage service, the liturgy of medieval England was entirely in Latin.

Worship in English was introduced at the time of the Reformation, in the sixteenth century, beginning with readings from the Bible at Morning and Evening Prayer (authorized in 1543), and the vernacular Litany in 1544, and culminating in the production of the first complete *Book of Common Prayer* in 1549, in the reign of Edward VI, Archbishop Thomas Cranmer being its chief architect. This contained full orders for Morning and Evening Prayer, the Eucharist (titled 'The Supper of the Lord and Holy Communion commonly called the Mass') together with its readings, and forms for baptism, confirmation and other services.

Because the **1549 Prayer Book** was a fairly conservative revision of the medieval texts, and the Eucharist in particular could still be interpreted in a traditional way, it did not satisfy the more radical reformers in the country. In **1552** a second English **Prayer Book** was authorized that was more decidedly Protestant in tone, the Eucharist now being called 'The Order for the Administration of the Lord's Supper or Holy Communion'. It was short-lived: when Edward VI died in 1553 and the Catholic Mary I came to the throne, the old Latin services were restored. In **1559**, a year after the accession of Elizabeth I, a slightly modified version of the 1552 book was authorized; a few minor additional changes were made in 1604, after James I had come to the throne.

After the outbreak of the Civil War in 1645, it was made illegal to use the Prayer Book in England. When the monarchy was restored in 1660, there were lively debates about the form in which the Prayer Book should also be restored. The outcome was a fresh revision, authorized by the Act of Uniformity of 1662. This **1662 Prayer Book**, with a few minor changes to some of the directions within it, remains in use to this day.

There was an unsuccessful attempt in 1927, and again in 1928, to introduce a revised version of the Prayer Book. Although Parliament rejected these attempts, the **1928 Prayer Book** was published and widely used, though it had no legal authority. Not until 1966 were experimental services alternative to those in the 1662 book authorized. A number of services were successively produced under the headings of Series 1, Series 2 and Series 3: **Series 1** was largely made up of parts of the rejected 1928 Prayer Book; **Series 2** was a set of new compositions based on more ancient patterns of service; and **Series 3** was a first attempt to put these into modern rather than Tudor English. The fruits of these experiments were revised into the ***Alternative Service Book* (ASB)** of 1980, which provided a complete set of services in modern English (together with a version of Holy Communion in traditional language), and was very widely used as an alternative to the 1662 Prayer Book for the next 20 years. Because authorization of the ASB was due to expire in 2000, and widespread use of it had revealed certain shortcomings, the Church of England embarked on a fresh process of liturgical revision in the 1990s. This led to the ***Common Worship*** series of services, authorized from 2000 onwards for use in the Church of England – always, like previous modern liturgies, as an alternative to, rather than a substitute for, the 1662 Prayer Book. Among other services, *Common Worship* provides a pattern for Holy Communion that follows the same basic structure as in the *ASB* (now known as Order One), and another that follows the basic structure of the service in the 1662 Prayer Book (known as Order Two). Either can be used in a modern-language or a traditional-language form.

Glossary

Advent	the season of the Christian year that precedes Christmas and prepares for the coming (Latin: *adventus*) of Jesus Christ
Apocrypha	those books that appear in the Old Testament of the earliest Christians (the authorized Greek translation of the Bible known as the Septuagint), and in the Vulgate Latin translation of the Bible, but do not appear in the traditional medieval text of the Hebrew Bible. The continental Reformers did not allow these 'extra' books to be included within their Bible. The Church of England allowed the apocryphal books to be used in worship and for ethics, but not for the definition of Christian doctrine
baptism	the rite by which new Christians are initiated into the Church. The person to be baptized is dipped or immersed in water, or has water poured over their head, 'in the name of the Father, the Son and the Holy Spirit'
breviary	a book containing the texts of all the daily 'hours of prayer' observed in monasteries, and by clergy, in the Middle Ages
canticle	a worship song, drawn either from the Bible or from other ancient sources
collect	a short prayer that gathers up or 'collects' the prayers of the people
compline	a service of night prayer, the last of the traditional services of the monastic day
creed	a statement of belief, from the Latin word *credo*: 'I believe'

doxology	an ascription of glory to God, normally as Father, Son and Holy Spirit, and usually forming the conclusion of a prayer or hymn
Eucharist	an ancient name widely used today for the service that is otherwise known as the Holy Communion, the Lord's Supper or the Mass
icon	an image (usually painted) of a biblical scene or person, or of a saint. In eastern orthodox tradition, the icon is a means through which honour and reverence can be given to what the icon represents
institution narrative	that part of a eucharistic prayer that recalls the words and actions of Jesus at the Last Supper. The words are a composite of New Testament texts, including St Paul's words in 1 Corinthians 11 (the earliest witness) as well as the accounts in the Gospels
intercessions	prayers made for other people, often by name
Joint Liturgical Group	a body of representatives from the main Christian denominations in the United Kingdom that has composed common worship material for use by any of its member churches
Lent	the season of the Christian year that prepares for Easter, modelled on the 40 days that Jesus spent in the wilderness after his baptism
litany	a form of **intercession** originating among eastern Christians and made up of a series of short prayer requests, each followed by a response said or sung by all
liturgy	in ancient Greece, a public work done by a citizen for the benefit of the people; in Christian usage, a term to denote public worship
Palm Sunday	the Sunday next before Easter, when Christians remember Jesus' triumphal entry into Jerusalem riding on a donkey. Palm Sunday opens the sequence of liturgies that make up Holy Week

Words for Worship

Pentecost   originally a Jewish festival on the fiftieth (Greek: *pentekoste*) day after the Passover, when the Holy Spirit is said to have descended on the Apostles (Acts 2), resulting in a Christian celebration of the gift of the Spirit on that day. Traditionally known in England as Whitsunday

petition   a request for God to act

vespers   a service of evening prayer; one of the traditional services of the monastic day

There are three Hebrew words that are often used in Christian worship that may be mentioned here. *Amen* is a response to a prayer, and means 'May it be so.' *Hallelujah* is an exclamation, and means 'Praise God!' It is often found in the Christianized form *Alleluia*. In Christian liturgy, it is especially an exclamation of Easter joy at the resurrection of Jesus, which is why there is a tradition of not using it during Lent. And *Hosanna*, which literally means 'Save now!' is in practice also an exclamation of praise.

To find out more

To find out more about the early history of Christian worship, a good place to start is Paul Bradshaw, *Early Christian Worship: A Basic Introduction to Ideas and Practice* (2nd edition. London: SPCK, 2010), or Paul Bradshaw and Maxwell Johnson, *The Origins of Feasts, Fasts, and Seasons in Early Christianity* (London: SPCK/Alcuin Club, 2011).

There is a classic *History of Anglican Liturgy* by Geoffrey J. Cuming (2nd edition London: Macmillan, 1982), which surveys the development of the *Book of Common Prayer*, and the early stages of liturgical revision in the Church of England. If you are interested in the detailed development of particular texts in the *Book of Common Prayer*, and have access to a library, then you could look at a *New History of the Book of Common Prayer... On the Basis of the Former Work by Francis Procter*, revised and rewritten by W. H. Frere (London: Macmillan, 1901, and long out of print).

For the 1980 ASB, see R. C. D. Jasper and Paul Bradshaw, *A Companion to the Alternative Service Book* (London: SPCK, 1986), and for *Common Worship* there is the parallel *Companion to Common Worship*, edited by Paul Bradshaw (2 volumes. London: SPCK/Alcuin, 2001, 2002).

The New SCM Dictionary of Worship, edited by Paul Bradshaw (London: SCM, 2002), is a useful reference work for everything to do with liturgy and worship.

There are many websites relevant to the prayers in this book. Here are some good starting-points:

www.transformingworship.org.uk is a direct way into all the Church of England's liturgical resources.

www.pbs.org.uk takes you to a wealth of material on the *Book of Common Prayer* and its place in the Church of England today.

www.commonworship.com takes you to the library of Common Worship texts.

www.oremus.org contains links to worldwide Anglican liturgical material.

Afterword

From the Bishop of Wakefield, The Rt Revd Stephen Platten, Chairman of the Liturgical Commission

One of the tried and tested ways of learning, even from our earliest years is to get to know something 'by heart'. Some parts of our experience become so well known to us that we need no book, no reminder of the text – we just know it by heart. This is true of so many parts of our lives. Our prayers and thanksgivings are no exception. So well known and so important for us are these that they become *landmarks* for us in living our lives. The *Lord's Prayer* (or *Our Father*) is perhaps the classical example, but there are others too. Certain parts of the Communion Service form other pieces of 'spiritual furniture' in our lives. Great musical settings of the Mass have made these texts more familiar still – the *Gloria*, the *Creed*, the *Sanctus* and the *Agnus Dei* have provided the libretto for some of the richest musical compositions over the centuries.

The Church of England has been an inheritor of these prayers and thanksgivings and they remain a rich treasury still. Over the centuries more prayers have been added to increase the store of riches available to us. In its different editions, the Book of Common Prayer goes back almost five hundred years, to the work of Thomas Cranmer at the Reformation – other prayers within it came later. Some of the phrases from this treasury have become part of our cultural and religious inheritance. Phrases are borrowed for book titles or used in our daily lives. For example 'Speak now or else hereafter for ever hold your peace.' and 'Cast away the works of darkness and put upon us the armour of light.' This book brings together just some of these prayers as well as giving us background to their origins and reflections as to their use.

These landmarks belong to us all. They are there for us to pray, to absorb and to inhabit. We may already know some *by heart*. If not then we might decide we want to learn them to 'carry around' with us in our hearts. In this way, these prayers may help fashion our lives and the lives of those whom we encounter.

Index

Index

Index